The Lost Village

The Lost Village

*Portrait of an
Irish Village in 1925*

John MacKenna

Dublin

The Lost Village
is published in 1995 by
New Island Books
2, Brookside,
Dundrum Road,
Dublin 14
Ireland

ISBN 1 874597 17 0

New Island Books receives financial assistance from
The Arts Council (An Chomhairle Ealaíon)
Dublin, Ireland.

This title was first published by the author under his own
imprint, Stephen Scroop Press, in Athy, Co. Kildare, in 1985,
and is here made available for the first time in a general trade
edition.

Cover design by Jon Berkeley
Printed in Ireland by Colour Books, Ltd.

Author's Note:

This is the story of one year – 1925 – in the history of the village of Castledermot in South Kildare. All of the events recorded happened. All of the people mentioned lived in the village. In some instances I have omitted names where their inclusion might cause embarrassment. I have, of course, reconstructed conversations – but only to illustrate verifiable events.

for Noel Lambe

I

Winter / Spring

John MacKenna

The news was spreading. From the Square in all directions, to Kempsey's Row, to the few men at Carey's Corner, to Dalton's pub and Doyle's and to the billiard hall. The Relieving Officer had been robbed on his way back to Athy. His car had been stopped beyond Kilkea and his money taken from him. Was he hurt? No one was sure. He might even be dead. Sergeant Scott got word of the robbery. He contacted the barrack in Athy. Yes there had been a hold up, but not a robbery. The Relieving Officer's car had broken down and he had had to walk the last few miles. The Sergeant relaxed, there had been enough trouble over the past few years. He was glad of the relative peace of 1925. There were summons papers to be served but for minor matters, nothing like armed robbery. Castledermot was a good place to be.

More slowly the word now spread that there had been no robbery. Some people seemed anxious not to believe the latest news, they could do with some excitement to brighten the dark, wet evening of the new year. What else was there to talk about - apart from politics and the eleven by-elections coming up in February. There was the more essential matter of the local elections promised for the Spring but few people expected those to go ahead. They had been postponed once already. They probably would be again.

A few men passed the billiard hall, walking carefully in the dark, wet street, making for home. It was no night for sitting on the bridge. The cold wind and sleety rain that had fallen regularly through 1924 was still falling. The men glanced up the steps passing the billiard hall but continued walking. At the gate of the parochial house they met the Parish Priest on his way to lock the church. They saluted him and disappeared into the darkness of Main Street.

Having locked the church, the P.P. checked the horses in the barn beside the church grounds. It was still early and he walked along Abbey Street, over Doyle's Bridge and onto the Carlow Road. A car was coming slowly down Barnhill, moving roughly on the pitted road that had deteriorated through the Winter. The priest waited in the shelter of Peter Hearns' wall until the car passed. It was Dr. Brannon, on his way back from a call. He was one of the few people in the village who owned a motor car. The P.P. was content with his horse and trap. He turned and went back the way he had come, past Hynes' and the Abbey and Joe Kinsella's, back to the quiet of the parochial house.

*　　　*　　　*

For those who had money there was an event to keep the Christmas spirit going into the first week of January. The Athy Farmers' Club was holding its annual dance on the first Wednesday of the new year but with tickets at 15 shillings for gentlemen and 12/6d for ladies the event was irrelevant to most people in the area. You could get a bargain, a pair of tickets for 25 shillings, but then the average week's wage for a labourer was thirty to forty shillings.

As the Great Southern and Western steam engine and carriages ground into Maganey station a Morris Cowley two seater pulled up in the yard outside. A few people got off the train. Some would travel by trap to Castledermot, some would walk to their homes. One young lady was being met by the owner of the Morris. He would take her back to his home, a large house on a farm of several hundred acres, and later they would travel to the Town Hall in Athy.

Turning the Morris onto the Levitstown road he passed four men cycling down into Maganey. They worked on his family farm six days a week. They would not be dancing in Athy.

*　　　*　　　*

The young man and his girl met other young farmers, a few clerks, a doctor and the sons and daughters of shopkeepers at the dance. There were one or two people from Castledermot but very few. They talked about the weather, the damage done to crops, about the young man's car - it had cost him £212. It was a low, sporty model in green and grey. He knew the others envied him. Twice he went to the window of the dancing hall to peer down on its dark shape in Emily Square. The band - the Adelaide Melody Band - played all the latest songs. In the supper room Mrs. Lawler of Naas oversaw the catering. It was a fine meal and the hall itself was a treat, decorated in sprays and posies of fresh flowers, arches of ribbon and crêpe paper and multicoloured lanterns.

"Let's hope the Spring picks up", someone said to him. "Otherwise the sowing is going to be ruined, just like the harvest".

"Have you seen the newspapers?"

"No."

"Six inches of rain in December alone, forty four inches in the year - the whole country is saturated. We need good, dry windy days for the next few weeks."

"That's not asking for a lot", the other man laughed.

*　　　*　　　*

In Mick Stanley's forge the blacksmith was working late. A few men and one boy sat watching the hammer catch a horse's shoe on the anvil. The bellows puffed and the light of the fire lit up the small forge.

"I'll tell you now", a man was saying. "I was in Athy there Monday at the market and I was looking for a coat, a good frieze overcoat and do you know how much they were asking?"

"How much?"

"Forty seven and six."

"It must've been gold lined."

"If it was itself they can keep it at that price."

The men were silent as the blacksmith lifted the tongs and dipped the heavy shoe in a barrel of water. A hiss of steam rose and then he held the curved metal in the firelight.

"That looks the job."

*   *   *

Driving home in the early hours of Thursday morning the Morris Cowley moved slowly on the bad roads. Frost glistened and there were pockets of snow in the dykes and ditches near Kilkea.

*   *   *

People began congregating in the yard of John Moore's farm in Plunketstown on the afternoon of Wednesday the 28th of January. It was a cold, showery day and most of those there were interested in furniture and bits and pieces of machinery. For a few, farmers themselves, the land was the object of their attendance.

"It's not bad land", one woman remarked to her husband.

He looked about him, non commital.

"I've seen worse", she persisted.

He nodded.

Another man came and joined them under the gable of the house.

"How's things?"

"All right. Trouble with bleddy dogs 'though."

"I seen that in the 'paper. Seems to be a rampage of them out Ballitore way."

"You can say that again", the man said. "I was up three nights last week. They got five sheep only down the road."

"Did you shoot any?"

"I did not", the man said, curling his lip. "But I will, if it's the last thing I do."

*   *   *

In the kitchen of the house two women were carefully examining a table and chairs. They looked for signs of woodworm. They pulled back the oilcloth that covered the table board and rubbed their hands on the grained timber.

"Not bad I suppose", the first woman said at last. "But it all depends on the price".

"Doyle'll get his price", the second commented. "They're not bringing him from Athy for nothin'. He'll get the last penny."

"Well, it won't be mine."

*   *   *

Four fields away a young boy, just out of school, was leading a team of horses through the drying earth. He was still awkward on the ploughed ground and he was thinking of that evening when he would write his letter answering an advertisement in the Nationalist for a shepherd on Cope's farm in Knocknagee. That might be the life, not this heavy handling of huge animals whose breath came down in icy clouds on his neck.

*   *   *

In Moone school the children were filing quietly out into the yard for their lunch. A man passing on his bicycle stopped and leaned on the wall as the Principal, Willie Doyle, crossed the mucky playground.

"Congratulations, Mister Doyle," he shouted. "I hear you were made a Peace Commissioner."

The 1st of February was a Sunday, a sometimes clear but mainly showery day. Some men were early on their bicycles, travelling to Carlow to hear the Minister for Home Affairs, Kevin O'Higgins, address a Cumann na nGael election rally at the Town Hall. It was a lunchtime gathering and the crowd were divided. Some had come from ten and fifteen miles away to hear the speech, others to heckle. In Castledermot itself the meeting and the political activities in the neighbouring county had brought old sores to the surface. At Cope's Corner and Doyle's Bridge people argued, sometimes bitterly, about O'Higgins and his policies on law and order. Others took the discussion back further, to the civil war of two years earlier. Hadn't a man been shot not ten yards from where they were standing, hadn't this Government sold them all out, wasn't there a need for law and order, wouldn't a united Ireland follow in time? The arguments had been heard over and over. Some people stayed to hear them out again. Others left and made for their houses, unwilling to fritter their one day of rest in trying to solve what couldn't be solved.

*   *   *

But politics and elections were not to be ignored. The local elections for the County Council were due in March. Meetings were being held every week. Cumann na nGael, Sinn Fein and the Labour Party were choosing their candidates, divisional meetings were held in Athy. The policies were hardly important - the issues were local. Work on improving the roads, for instance, had slowed because of the lack of money. Men were being let go because the Council did not have money to pay them. The party which could solve that problem would get the votes.

*   *   *

In the fields and on the farms around Castledermot the pace of life was increasing. At Cope's mill in Prumplestown farmers were arriving to collect sacks of seed oats and barley. Their carts and traps and trailers travelled from Graney and Kilkea and Levitstown to collect the crop seeds, meeting on the tight bend at the Mill Pond. At the Mill itself work went busily on. The huge wooden wheel turned, dripping the waters of the Lerr as it powered the machinery inside. Pulleys raised and lowered the hundredweight sacks. Trailers were loaded and driven to Maganey for the up and down trains. And, in the slowly brightening evenings, men cycled home from the mill to begin work on tilling their own gardens.

*   *   *

What had been an improving Spring suddenly became Winter again on the morning of Saturday, February 8th. For two hours in the early morning, between three and five, a blizzard raged in the village and the people woke to inches of snow on the streets and drifts in the doorways. The veranda of O'Connell's house, in the Main Street, was powdered heavily with snow, it lay damply on the thatched roof of Thorpe's, across the road, and in the doorway of the Post Office. Mrs. Cross was busy sweeping it clear and in the Square Dan MacEvoy was clearing the snow and slush from the platform around the water pump. A few children threw snowballs at him from behind the ouncel house and then ran away, down Athy Street. Gardens that had been dug were buried beneath the heavy fall. A few men, warmed by their early morning drink, looked out of the window of Aylmer's pub at the people coming carefully across the School Lane.

"Sooner them nor me", one remarked and turned again to his glass of whiskey.

On the farms the plough horses stayed in their stables and the farmers wondered what else could happen - first the rain through the Winter and now, just when things were breaking, this snowstorm.

For Daisy Dent, dressmaker, work went on snow or shine. In her tiny cottage tucked in above the Fair Green she was cutting and sewing dresses for the commercial dance, now less than two weeks away. Business was steady but something like this helped to boost her earnings. It might stop others working but the snow was no trouble to her.

*   *   *

For some of the children in Kempsey's Row and the cottages in the School Lane the snow was a mixed blessing. It meant games to play but it also meant they'd have to spend an extra week in shoes. And for some it meant school in barefeet anyway, snow or not.

*   *   *

The rows of bikes along the wall on Barrack Street and the carts and traps in the Square and down to the Fair Green made it clear that this was court day. Men and women stood about uneasily in their Sunday clothes, solicitors consulted with their clients outside the bank on the Square. In the Leinster Arms men gulped a quick drink and looked up at the clock, preparing themselves for the worst. The courtroom itself was crowded with people, chattering quietly, waiting apprehensively. In the side room District Justice Liam Price was robing. He could hear the coughing and sneezing from the room outside. He checked, again, that he had all his papers and then signalled to the clerk that he was ready to begin. The side door opened and the clerk called on those in the court to stand. Price walked up the steps to his bench, closing the wooden gate behind him. and settled himself for a day of minor cases.

Unlit bicycles, a dozen cases of farmers who had allowed their hedges to go uncut through the Spring, causing a nuisance to passing traffic. Mr.

Rorke, the County Surveyor, had brought the cases. Orders were made. Next was a case of assault. One man had called another a scab for taking his job as a farm labourer, blows had been struck.

"The blow wouldn't hurt a baby", the defendant claimed.

He was warned and fined.

A man who lived in a council cottage in Prumplestown was in arrears of rent to the tune of three pounds five shillings. He had been warned, the council solicitor claimed, but had made no attempt to pay and had no means of doing so. The council wished to have an eviction order made against the man. The justice agreed. Sergeant Scott recounted the arrest of a local man who had been drunk and disorderly after the closing of the public houses.

"I warned him", the Sergeant said. "He told me he was a Republican and he didn't care about the Civic Guards. He was very abusive and his language was very rough. He resisted me."

The justice delivered a lecture on the importance of respect for the police force and consideration for people in their beds at that hour of the night.

"Fined two pounds or a month in jail", he concluded.

The court broke for lunch. A tray of food was brought for the justice. The Sergeant went home. Those who had got off lightly made for home or went to MacEvoy's tearooms. The man who had been fined the £2 was a hero. He sat sipping a drink in Kelly and Byrne's public house.

After lunch the cases continued. The lights came on in the court room, fines were handed out, warnings given. No one went to jail - this time.

"Is that it?", the justice asked as the list reached its end.

"There's one other thing", Sergeant Scott said, rising uneasily. "On behalf of the Court staff and myself I'd like to congratulate you on your recent wedding and wish you and your bride happiness and long years of health."

"Thank you very much", the justice smiled.

Driving out the Dublin Road he hoped he wasn't coming down with 'flu, it was hard to avoid when you sat for hours in stuffy courtrooms.

*   *   *

On the Monday and Tuesday of the fourth week in February there was a stream of women calling to Daisy Dent to collect their dresses for the commercial dance on the Tuesday night. She made last minute adjustments and repairs to the frocks and then saw the women off. Minutes later someone else would arrive. In Cope's shop, in Thompson's hardware and in Paddy Nolan's public house young men and women were looking forward to the night's celebration. The members of the organizing committee were at the dancehall early in the afternoon. Mrs. Lawler and her staff arrived from Naas just after tea time. This was a particularly special night. Months of work had gone into the building of this co-operative hall and now it stood, completed, opposite Kelly's public house, set back from the road. From nine o' clock onwards the village was alive. Bicycles were parked in the yard beside the dancehall. Traps drew up outside Walsh's and Jimmy Doyle's, depositing stylishly dressed women. Then they moved off again, to be parked on the Fair Green.

Inside the hall the music was filling the dance room, the supper room and the cloak rooms.

"Who's the band?"

"O Rourke's Orchestra of Carlow."

"They're good.

"Not bad at all."

The first sitting of supper was underway. Those with tickets for the second sitting danced on the spacious floor.

The music lasted into the early hours, spot prizes were won, those who had not bought tickets stood about outside, waiting to catch a glimpse of the style as the hall emptied.

In the ticket kiosk committee members counted the takings.

"Two hundred and sixty people, give or take a few. That's not bad."

"Not bad at all. Didn't I say it'd be a success."

*   *   *

Walking or cycling or driving home in the small hours all kinds of things were discussed. The band, of course, and the catering. The floor of the dancehall. The news that the local elections had, definitely, been postponed by the government. The new fad for doing crosswords - even the Nationalist was carrying a weekly puzzle. The riot in Maryborough jail - had people heard about it? Very rough.

*   *   *

For some of those who had loitered outside, the night had been passed in walking about the town, looking in shop windows. Examining the bicycles in Hennessy's window. Seven pounds twelve and sixpence for a new bike - hire purchase terms available.

"I'll tell you now what I was thinking", one shop boy commented. "I'll never get the money for a new bike but I might get together the price of one of them three speed gears. You can put them on your own bike."

"The Stormey three speed?"

"Yeah."

"How much?"

"A Guinea."

"That's a fair few bob."

"But they're bleddy great."

The agricultural night classes, which had run through the Winter, came to an end that same week. Mr. Cawley, who had travelled from Athy to give them, was thanked for his help. Everyone agreed they had been a great help.

"You'll be moving over here no doubt soon", one woman commented to him as the class stood about.

"Why's that?"

"When they turn the fever 'ospital into one for T.B. patients. You'll all be leavin' then."

"You might be right there. Nobody wants T.B. in the middle of the town."

"Are you goin' to do anythin' about it?"

"I hear there's some kind of committee being got together but you never know with these things."

*   *   *

Dr. Bannon walked back to his car. He had driven to Athy to collect his newly made lounge suit from Shaws. It had cost him five guineas.

*   *   *

Tuesday, February 24th, was Fair day in Castledermot. From dawn the cattle jobbers and horse traders, the huxters and stall holders had been arriving in the Square. Setting up their stalls on the Main Street, down Keenan's Lane, past Ivor's Lane and onto the Green. Byrne's and Mac Evoy's were packed as they catered for farmers and dealers in search of a meal. The public houses were full to overflowing. There were ballad sellers, clothes sellers, dealers in china and delf ware, three card trick men, farmers, labourers, horse dealers, poultry sellers and country people mixing with the villagers. At times it was impossible to move through the throng. Sergeant Scott walked about, keeping a wary eye on things. There had been one short scuffle near Tommy Dwyer's house but he had been able to sort it out quickly and send the two men involved on their way. In MacEvoy's and Byrne's plates piled with cabbage, potatoes and bacon were passed over the heads of diners to men and women in the corner seats. Mike Hennessy had sold three bicycles. There was a flurry of excitement after lunch. One of the Ladies Fitzgerald had driven in from Kilkea and her trap was moving slowly up Barrack Street.

In Aylmer's pub someone had struck up a local ballad about another event:

> On the 24th February the boys they did agree
> to go up to Daniel Synott's that night in Knocknacree.
> The boys arrived at half past nine, no music did they hear,
> but sure it was for poor old Danny them all began to cheer...

Dan Murphy had worked particularly hard to get extra bread to the shops for this fair day and he was preparing for a trip to Hannon's mill to replenish his flour. Cope's bakery had sold out its stocks. While his wife served meals all day Willie Byrne had been mending and selling saddles and harnesses to farmers. Mick Stanley was still working in his forge. Mat Lawler had taken in dozens of pairs of shoes in his house near Carlow Gate and would cobble them over the next two weeks. MacDonald's butcher's shop was open late, selling to those who were making a day of the Fair. Still open, too, was Dalton's grocery, on the corner of School Lane and Abbey Street. The last business of the day was being concluded. Most of the horses and cattle had been taken away but a few were penned or tethered in the timbered boxes at the end of Keenan's Lane.

*   *   *

The blizzard of early February seemed to have cleared the Winter weather and the early part of March was warm and dry. With the late improvement the ploughing and seeding, which had been held up by the heavy rains, got underway. The school attendance fell off and young boys led horses for teenage farm labourers; the older, more experienced, hands ploughed other fields alone - putting the reins over one shoulder and round under the other arm and gripping the plough with both hands. One hand on the plough, the other managing the reins, these men turned the horse on the headland and ploughed slowly back as they had come.

Lambing was well under way, shepherds working late and early to deliver flocks safely. The job in Cope's had been filled. In the village gardens the interrupted digging and sowing had resumed. Those with no work to do in the evenings or without the will to do it met to play football or pitch and toss at the end of Keenan's Lane. Others sat on Doyle's Bridge and talked until only the reddening tips of their cigarettes could be seen in the twilight.

"We won't see the evenings lengthening now. The boys are back at footballin' already."

"You wouldn't have believed it a couple of weeks back."

"They're even talkin' about cricket out in Hallahoise an' we not at Easter yet."

*   *   *

There had been practise dances in the new hall in February and early March but the event of St. Patrick's night was the dance in Ballitore town hall. Men and women with bunches of shamrock wilting on their coats cycled the few miles to be there. There was one regret. They had expected the Castledermot Dance Band - Pat Hennessy, John Byrne and Willie and James Tierney - to play but instead a local orchestra had been employed.

The cyclists passed in groups through Moone and Timolin, appraising the newly ploughed fields. Laughing and shouting to each other. Hurrying to catch familiar figures in the distance. Two women were discussing the new dancehall in Castledermot.

"It's nice but there was something about the girl's school I liked.'

"It wasn't as big."

"No, but it was grand to go across to the billiard hall for the supper and then come back to more dancing. It was like going out twice on the one night."

In Ballitore the hall was crowded. People danced 'till six o'clock the next morning and many cycled straight to work.

Coming home the dancers noticed several dogs and cats dead on the road between Ballitore and Timolin. In the night someone had spread poison on the roadway. A fox was dead too - the Kildare Hounds had assembled that morning at 11 o'clock on the Square in Athy.

* * *

In Bolger's of Main street a card game was ending.

"It's near time to give the cards a rest, the weather is gettin' too fine", Mrs. Giltrap, the butcher, said.

A few people nodded.

"There's never a time you can't have a hand of cards", Billy Hoey, the shoemaker, laughed.

"Begod, if we don't get our extra few shillin's we may give up playin' ", a man said from the corner of the kitchen.

"Will yis?"

"It's not lookin' good. The Council says they can't afford it."

"Aren't you doin' alright", another man said, winking. "Thirty bob is more than yer worth."

"You're not lookin' for a lot - ten bob no less", Billy Hoey laughed.

"There's no harm in lookin' but I don't thing we'll be gettin'."

"I see in the paper", Mrs. Giltrap said, "that they're saying there's no money for the upkeep of the roads. They're saying they might get some in the next month."

"Begod, Dr. Bannon'll be glad to hear that, the bones are shook out of him drivin' around in his motor car."

* * *

In farm houses around the village work started earlier and earlier now. Spring was truly here, the snow and sleet laid to rest. Occasionally there were bites of frost in the morning but the sun cleared these quickly and by half past eight, the procession of barefooted children making for the village schools attested to the end of Winter. The horses were working every day. Stanley's and Wall and Butler's forges were busy from early morning. For the shoemakers of the village and for Jimmy Loughlin, who sold turf from his house on the Green, times were less busy now that Summer was around the corner. Tompsie Lawler was busy in his garden at the Turnpike, putting in cabbage plants. Mrs. Owens looked from the windows of the Leinster Arms at the children swinging on the chains around the pump in the Square. At Carlow Gate other children played marbles and every evening there were shouts to be heard from the football field on Dempsey's land at Barn Hill. Mike Hennessy was expanding his business and had begun work as an auctioneer.

*   *   *

It was three o'clock in the morning when Paddy Nolan, asleep over his pub in Main street, was awakened by the banging on the door of Nurse Gannon's house. It was across the road from his own. The nurse went with the man who had come for her. She did not return for several hours. In the house to which she had gone the woman had lost a premature baby.

"What will you do?" the nurse asked the woman's husband as she left.

"I could bury it in the garden but maybe not."

"Are the others buried there?"

"Yes, it seems odd but what else can we do?"

Nurse Gannon nodded.

"I'll see if I can get someone."

It was a cold, bright morning when the nurse got back to her house. There was movement in Sam Wright's shop next door.

An hour later the man to whom she had spoken cycled with a neighbour, out of the village, through Hallahoise and down Mullaghcreelan. Clipped on the back carrier of his bike was a box. Inside, wrapped in a sheet, was the body of his child. The other man carried a shovel. They buried the child in a field that had once held the ruins of a church. Then they cycled back to Castledermot and on to work.

II

Spring / Summer

Palm Sunday, the first Sunday of April, was a warm, clear day. The courting couples and families out walking the roads around Castledermot and those seeking the greater seclusion of the fields above the Cuckoo Steps and across to Mullarney were surprised by the profusion of primroses in the ditches.

A week of Church ceremonies lay ahead and after them the end of Lent and a return to festivities. Castledermot Carnival Dance was being talked about. Manahan's Band was travelling from Dublin to provide the music on Easter Sunday night. Good Friday, the tenth of April, was a day of fasting. Little or no work was done on the land or in the shops and businesses of the village. For some of the older people in the village the old beliefs still held - no work could be done, no animals killed, no nails driven, no timber burned. The vast majority thronged to the church for the ceremonies at three in the afternoon and many returned that night. Visits were made to St. James' graveyard. Despite tradition, the day was fine and hot, and in many yards and gardens boys and men were having their hair cut, to ward off headaches in the coming year.

Easter Saturday continued warm. The shops were open again. Kelly's workshop hummed; Martha Nolan, the Principal of the girl's school travelled to Carlow and bought herself a pair of patent leather shoes for 16/11; Cope and Torry's was crowded with young girls buying bits and pieces to set off their new dresses; Thompson's hardware shop was busy; in his house, at the Turnpike, Sam Brown, the Methodist preacher, was preparing the sermon he would deliver to his congregation the following day; in the billiard hall those waiting for a game were discussing the Athy billiard final to which most had travelled on Palm Sunday to see D.W. Walsh beat Tommy Miles; in the Catholic church the queues grew outside the confession boxes.

*   *   *

The Easter ceremonies were not alone the highlight of the church calendar but also an opportunity for people to show their style. Heads glistened with hair oil, newly bought shoes squeaked noisily. For those in tune with what was highly fashionable the knitted costume was in vogue, particularly, in pale and brick colours. Most had bought their clothes in Athy or Carlow, one or two had travelled further afield. The continuing heat made the costumes uncomfortable, however, and the women who had opted for lighter frocks found the service a more comfortable experience.

Relaxing on Easter Sunday morning, after early Mass, many people read with interest the long article in the Nationalist on the history of

Castledermot. It had been written in 1913 by the Rev. Vandeleur, then rector at Kilkea, and gave a thorough account of the history of the village. It concluded:

> "Although there are poor dwellings still to be seen yet these are disappearing and their place being taken by neat labourer's cottages and prosperous-looking shops. May it be the ambition of each dweller in this famous old town to do something to make the present worthy of its past: may the spirit of brotherliness and friendliness which now reigns in Castledermot continue always and spread through the land."

*　　　*　　　*

Brotherliness was the theme, too, of a meeting held in Castleroe on Easter Sunday afternoon. Organised by the local section of the Irish Transport and General Workers' Union, it was to finalise plans for the upcoming local elections which would take place on June 23rd.

Jim Foley, the area organiser for the union, and himself a candidate in the election, addressed the meeting. He referred to the recent, unsuccessful farm labourers' strike and the return of men to the union in recent times. He hoped the whole area would soon be re-organised. When the union was organised in 1918 the farm workers were treated like slaves by the farmers, he said.

> "They paid low wages 'though they could afford good wages, times were good for them. It was the union forced them to. I'm glad for that reason, that there's such a good crowd here today. It's important that we're organised now because we're being attacked from all sides. No other union fought harder for workers and, of course, we're bound to have losses as well as gains. It's no good men leaving a union when they're defeated, that's the time to band together and fight again. As long as we're disorganised we'll never get anything. And it's important, too, to look after the organising of the unemployed - and there's plenty of them in this area. Giving last year's grants the government cut back on money because they thought they could get away with it, that there was so many unemployed. Are men out of work not entitled to a decent living too?

> We have a good committee to organise for this election. We have good men standing. We have to make sure we get every working person to vote Labour because the Labour Party is the only one to look after the working class. We kept the Council men's wages up for the coming year, no other party would've done that."

Foley's words were greeted with claps and shouts of approval. **Mick Smyth**, a Labour county councillor, pointed out that the Labour Party was carrying its message across the country. They had good men standing in this area, men who would fight for shorter working hours for the farm labourer, for better pay, for protection against accidents at work. All the worker had was his labour, he wanted the highest price possible for it.

Those who had attended the meeting came away elated. They had heard stirring speeches, they believed they could do well in the local elections. The farmer candidates might have money behind them but the workers had numbers.

* * *

While farmers and labourers prepared to face each other in the June election they worked side by side on the land. In Woodlands East Billy Brown was laying poison on his fields; Copes of Knocknagee were preparing for the sale of part of their pedigree large white pigs and at Wright's of Prumplestown sales of Arran Chief and Shamrock seed potatoes was steady. Mike Hennessy's auctioneering was steady too. In the week after Easter he had two properties for sale. The first was a twenty five acre holding at Garterfarm and the second a parcel of ten acres at Coolane. Both holdings were being sold by the Irish Land Commission.

* * *

The carnival dance on Easter Sunday night was a huge success and was followed on Easter Monday evening by the opening of a show that was to run for seven nights at the new hall. Posters in the village gave all the details:

THE NEW HALL, CASTLEDERMOT
FRANK DALTON
Late producer Queen's Theatre, Dublin
PRESENTS HIS IRISH PLAYERS
for seven nights only opening
EASTER MONDAY APRIL 13th
with
THE PERIL OF SHEILA
The rollicking romantic Irish costume drama
Caste includes
MISS ANNIE MULHALL OF CARLOW
the Irish contralto and

C. WISEMAN LESLIE
Ireland's favourite comedian and entertainer
Performance concludes each night with
the concert and screaming farce
Complete change of programme nightly
PRICES: 9d; 1/3d; 2/4d   Doors open 8 o'clock sharp

All seats were filled for the week. The local shopkeepers and teachers filling the front rows, the labourers sitting at the back.

*   *   *

Dr. Bannon, with several other doctors in the area, was becoming alarmed at the increase in the number of cases of tuberculosis The suggestion of turning the fever hospital in Athy into a centre for treating T.B. had, at first, been treated as a subject for discussion. Now everyone in the village knew of somebody who had contracted the disease. Seven years earlier influenza had been the great killer. Now it seemed another plague was about to strike. An urgent meeting of Athy urban council was called to discuss the question of the hospital. In Castledermot several houses had victims of T.B. For most of those who contracted the disease it was fatal.

Several times during that Spring funeral processions made their way from the church, past the girls' school and right at Aylmer's public house, down Church lane to St. James' graveyard. On these occasions the Catholic population would enter the grounds of the Church of Ireland and make for the open grave in the Catholic section. On other occasions, when a member of the Church of Ireland community died, people would stand outside the gates, watching from a distance but not going in.

As the daffodils bloomed in the shadow of the round tower and the birds hatched in the trees around the graveyard wall priest and minister, in turn, prayed over members of their congregation who had died of T.B.

*   *   *

Out in the fields the barley shoots were up, proving that the severe Winter and wet Spring had had no effect. In some areas farmers had set aside a few acres to grow sugar beet for test purposes. They had been advised that sugar beet was the coming crop, that the area would be a centre for the development of a beet and sugar industry.

*   *   *

On Sunday the nineteenth of April Hennessy's car was hired to take some stalwarts to the Leinster hurling championship match between Kildare and Leix. It was a one sided affair. Leix won by eight goals and four points to one goal and one point. The next day saw most of the farmers and many shopkeepers on their way to Athy for the South Kildare Agricultural Society horse jumping competitions. The grey and green Morris Cowley was among the cars parked at the Showgrounds. Starting at three o 'clock the jumping got underway with an inter-hunt competition. This was followed by the ladies cup and then the open sweepstakes, for which the winning rider received 2/3d. and the second and third competitors 1/3d. The show ended with a closed competition for farmers and residents of Athy. Apart from the jumping there were all kinds of sideshows in the grounds and the large crowd enjoyed the sunshine and bustle.

*   *   *

For Michael Whelan of Kilkea, however, the week was not so pleasant. John Conlan, T.D., had raised a question in the Dail asking the Minister for Lands if he was aware that Michael Whelan had been evicted from his holding of 18 acres on the Verschoyle estate in 1903 and had, since, been trying for reinstatement. The Minister said he was. Conlan pursued the matter, pointing out that the lands were now being divided by the Land Commission and requesting the immediate reinstatement of Michael Whelan. The Minister was not impressed.

"The Commissioners have enquired into and considered Michael Whelan's application and have decided not to take action in that respect", he said.

"On what grounds was the decision come to?" Conlan asked.

"This man was evicted in 1903 and I understand he is over 80 years of age and has no relatives", the Minister answered.

"Haven't persons evicted prior to 1903 been reinstated?"

"Yes but the circumstances in this case don't warrant reinstatement", the Minister said finally.

*   *   *

The last Sunday in April saw two different but equally attractive events. The parish Catholic retreat opened with Mass. Stalls, filled with rosary beads and medallions, were set up near the church. The missioners preached hellfire and brimstone sermons, guaranteeing a packed church and long lines outside the confessionals. But on the same day dozens of men from the parish travelled to Dublin to be among the 30,000 crowd in Croke Park to see Kerry beat Dublin by four points to three in the All Ireland football final.

Trains from Athy and Maganey were full of eager fans. Others had clubbed together to hire a car from Hennessy's or Farrelly's. Bicycles were parked three and four deep against the wall of the station house in Maganey. Those who had made the journey saw an exciting, if unspectacular, game.

*   *

While the mission continued through the week meetings were held and the local people were canvassed for their votes as the local elections drew nearer.

*   *   *

May Day was an important one on the land. Cattle which had been kept in byres and stall fed were turned out on the fresh grass. A board dance had been planned for the Fair Green but May swept in like a lion with hail, rain and bitter cold. It seemed this year would never see the end of last year's Winter.

The bad weather helped to swell the numbers who enrolled for the evening classes arranged by the county vocational education committee. On Tuesday nights a reasonable number of men gathered for woodwork and on Wednesdays a large number of women attended the domestic economy and cookery sessions.

The second Sunday of the month saw a huge crowd in the new hall as Mr. Bramley of Athy presented the first of his twice weekly cinema entertainments.

"Nothing but up to date and clean pictures will be thrown on the screen", he assured his audience.
The crowd took him at his word and packed the hall, again, on Thursday night. The moving picture business had arrived to stay.

*   *   *

On Wednesday the 13th of May District Justice Price was back in Castledermot for the district sessions.

A young man from the village, who had been charged with falsely collecting money from unemployment insurance while working, sat at the back of the court, waiting for the Justice to appear.

"Don't worry about it", his father assured him. "He's not the worst. He won't go too hard on you."

The solicitor representing the young man apologised on his behalf, pointing out that his client was prepared to repay the money.

The judge listened and then looked up: "Imprisonment for one month without hard labour", he said. "Next case."

Guard Hanrahan summoned a man from Belan who was charged with driving a motor cycle at Castledermot on May 9th without a silencer. The man was fined 5s. The cases progressed. An order for repossession of a house at Prumplestown - the same case which had come up at the previous session. A local farmer summoned a young girl from Castledermot for damaging fences and taking wood off his land at Corballis. Mr. Byrne, solicitor, appearing for the complainant, said the farmer had found the girl on his land. He was having trouble with people entering his land and destroying his fences and wanted it to end.

The girl was called into the witness box.

"I was only takin' a few bits of sticks", she said vehemently. "I never done no damage to any fences."

The Justice ordered the girl's father to pay a fine of sixpence and six shillings expenses.

"He's in a bloody rough humour today", a woman at the door remarked.

A long case took up most of the afternoon. Kildare County Council were seeking an order to allow them entry to a gravel pit at Barnhill, the property of Miss Cope. The Assistant Surveyor, Mr. Hurley, pointed out that this was the only pit in the district capable of supplying the material for roadmaking.

Mr. Byrne, Miss Cope's solicitor, cut in: "Miss Cope has been supplying material for the roads for a long time?"

"Yes", Hurley said.

"Without any court order?"

"Yes."

"What provision have you made for taking account of the material taken out?"

"The ganger is there every day".

"I'm not here to fix the value today", the Justice said testily.

"I'm merely trying to insure my client is not robbed", Byrne replied.

John Donohoe, the ganger, was called and stated that he kept an account of the loads taken from the pit.

Mr. Rorke, the County Surveyor, told the Justice the material was required for tar painting. The material was in the pit but Miss Cope would not allow the men into the pit.

"I'm anxious to see the landowner paid", Rorke said. "But I can't promise to pay what we have been paying. The money isn't there. We have paid the owner of this pit generously", he added. "She received £100 last year."

"You forgot to say you did not pay her for what you took out", Miss Cope's solicitor interjected.

"We've paid her too much already", Rorke replied angrily.

Miss Cope herself was called and told the Justice the pit had been used for generations and given freely but the Council had no way of checking what material was being taken out. She was also worried about the amount of trespass on the land. Finally, Justice Price made an order in favour of the Council and complimented the county surveyor on the way the roads were maintained. He would settle the question of value later.
"It's my experience", he concluded, "that this material is needed badly. The Castledermot to Carlow road needs tarring very badly now. I know, I drive on it."

Two orders for repossession of houses on local farms were made and a tranfer of licence for the premises of the late Mr. Byrne was made, temporarily, to Patrick Nolan.

*   *   *

The court session over, life went on. Thursday night saw another picture show. Across Woodlands the corncrake could be heard croaking. At Cope's corner people gathered and shared news of relatives in Birmingham. Mr. & Mrs. Flaherty went about their business of teaching, he in the two storied boys' school beside their house at the School lane, she in the girls' school at the other end of the lane. On the eaves of houses and under the thatch of Thorpe's roof the swallows were nesting.

*   *   *

The Church of Ireland community were about to have their parish mission. On the 17th May it opened. It was conducted by the Rev.

Batterby of St. Mary's parish in London. There were sermons at half past eight, noon and five o'clock on the opening day and at ten o'clock each morning through the week. In Kinneigh and Kilkea Rev. Batterby preached twice during the week. The turnout was large. Catholic children hid in the Laurels, watching through the trees as cars and traps drew up at the church gates and people made their way inside. Once the service had begun they made their way to the wall of the churchyard. They did not venture any further.

*　　　*　　　*

Yet again, the weather had improved and the tennis club was a popular meeting place. In the evenings there were several gatherings to play meggars. On the last Sunday of the month a squad of cyclists travelled to Carlow to see Kildare play Carlow in the football championship. It was a one sided affair. The Kildare goalkeeper spent a quarter of an hour of the first half and all of the second leaning against his goalpost, arms folded.

"If the rest of the matches are as handy as that we'll be alright", a man said cycling in by Cope's Mill.

"If they're that handy we'll never keep awake", his companion replied. They passed two men cycling in the opposite direction.

"Yis weren't at the match!"

"No, we had an election meetin'. Who won?"

"Kildare."

*　　　*　　　*

There were two men from the immediate locality contesting the election. One was John Dunne. He was a farm labourer and lived in a cottage in Barnhill West. He was representing the Labour party. The second was John Nassau Greene of Kilkea Lodge. He was a farmer, representing the farmers' and ratepayers' group. Among the local workers and labourers there was no doubt about who would receive first preference but the shopkeepers and landowners were suspicious of the Labour movement, they would opt for their own.

*　　　*　　　*

Summer was truly here. Every night now the roads around Castledermot were a hive of activity. Badminton players cycling to Tullow to play; footballers on their way to Barnhill; courting couples at Knocknacree;

33

pitch and toss schools at Keenan's Lane; groups on their way to the Picture Palace in Athy to see a concert.

Those going by car had reserved their seats at 3/6d each. Others would take the second seats at 2/3d. For most the 1/3d admission would suffice.

*   *   *

On the second Sunday in June, John Dunne travelled to Athy to attend a meeting addressed by Tom Johnston, T.D., the Labour Party leader. A large crowd gathered in the Square. John Dunne stood, slightly self consciously on the platform. The main thrust of Johnston's speech dealt with unemployment and the Labour party's attempt to help the unemployed. Turning to local matters Johnston promised help with the Barrow drainage and urged the people of Athy, Castledermot and Ballitore to support their local Labour party candidates.

Travelling home Dunne was overtaken by some men from Castledermot.

"Do you think you'll do well?"

"I'll do my best. It's hard to tell what way it'll go."

"You have our vote anyway."

*   *   *

On the same day the Forty Hours ceremonies began in Castledermot Catholic Church. The principal celebrants were the local curate, Fr. Condon, and the Parish Priest, Fr. Carrol. A procession took place through the church grounds with the local sodality group, the school children and altar boys taking part. The choir was conducted by Mr. Flaherty.

*   *   *

Voting was slow on election day. Sergeant Scott and Guard Hanrahan oversaw the polling. People came in ones and twos. There was little enthusiasm throughout the morning and afternoon. The tallymen outside the booth had little to do until six o'clock when a rush of voters began and went on through the next hour until just after seven.

The voters were faced with an array of candidates:

    Corcoran, Thomas: Athy; Gentleman.
    Dunne, John: Castledermot; Labourer.
    Fennell, Wm. James: Athy; Farmer.
    Flynn, James: Athy; Farmer.

Foley, James: Athy; Trades Union Secretary.
Foley, Patrick: Ballitore; Labourer.
Greene, John Nassau: Kilkea: Farmer.
Henderson, George W.: Athy; Farmer.
Keegan, James: Athy; Farmer.
Malone, Michael: Athy; Merchant.
Supple, C.J.:Athy; Labourer.

The five seats for the electoral area would be filled from the eleven men fighting the contest.

Once the rush of voters was over the tallymen returned to their leisurely conversation. When the polls closed Sergeant Scott and Guard Hanrahan oversaw the sealing of the boxes and travelled with them to Athy where they would be counted on Wednesday. John Dunne sat with his friends on the wall at the corner of Church Lane. Some of those passing homeward in the twilight wished him well in the count.

"We'll see how it goes", he said.

* * *

It was late afternoon when John Dunne reached the count centre in Athy. He had been working through the day. The Athy Urban Council count had been made and the Presiding Officer, Michael Doyle, was checking the votes for the County Council election. The first count result was announced. There were 121 spoiled votes. Dunne was very pleased. He was fifth after the first count with 283 votes, six votes ahead of Greene. William Fennel had headed the poll and been elected. Castledermot had voted strongly for Dunne. His friends told him he was in with a chance. Pat Foley of Ballitore was below him if he was eliminated he might push Dunne towards a seat. Fennell's surplus vote made no difference to the situation and Dunne watched anxiously as Supple and Keegan were eliminated and their votes distributed. Keegan transferred heavily to Corcoran and gave him the second seat. Pat Foley and Michael Malone were next to go. Dunne got a fair share of Foley's transfers but not enough to put him in. Malone, the Athy shopkeeper, transferred strongly to Henderson, the Athy farmer, giving him the third seat. There were now three men left chasing two seats: Nassau Greene, James Foley and Dunne. Dunne was bottom of the three and was eliminated. His votes were transferred, putting Foley ahead of Greene. Both of these were elected without reaching the quota.

George Henderson immediately proposed a vote of thanks to the returning officer and his staff. The vote was seconded by W.G. Doyle on behalf of William Fennell. The other three men elected associated themselves with the proposal and the crowd began to disperse.

In the street outside the Ballyroe pipe band was playing.

John Dunne collected his bicycle and travelled home, pleased that he had done so well but disappointed that he hadn't taken the fifth seat. Next time, perhaps.

*   *   *

The last Sunday in June saw a match in the Sunday Cricket League at Hallahoise. A few people walked and cycled out from Castledermot to sit on the ditch beside Lamb's and watch the local team play their first home game.

It was a tempestuous affair. Tempers were frayed and the local umpire was challenged on more than one occasion about his failure to give LBW decisions against the Kilkea batsmen. The local men stayed at the wickets until late in the afternoon, making 86 runs before their tenth wicket fell. Their bowlers gave the more polished players from the Athy Gentlemen's club a lot of trouble in the early overs and looked set to win but by the time the sun was dipping behind the trees towards Greene's yard Athy were overhauling them and going on to win by two wickets. The last ball was bowled in twilight. By then the spectators had gone home.

"Next week, one o'clock, we'll meet down at the bridge."

"Who are we playing?"

"Athy Players."

"Not this crowd again."

"No, the other Athy team. They're better than this lot but they're not so full of rubbish. They won't have accents that'd knock you down anyway."

"Right. I'll see you Tuesday night anyway."

"Good luck."

III

Summer / Autumn

John MacKenna

The Summer of 1925 was as good as most people could remember. True, the Winter had dragged well into Spring but now that the fine weather had come it seemed destined to last indefinitely. Go out any road and you could see hay in tramp cocks, field after field of it.

Another crop, however, was exercising the minds of local farmers, workers, politicians and businessmen - beet. Everywhere it was being talked about. For farmers, in particular, it was all consuming. But everyone was concerned. The date for the announcement of a site for the new sugar beet factory was imminent. Local opinion had been at one on the general area - it must be in the Barrow Valley. But local opinion had been divided on where the exact siting should be - Carlow and Athy were the two most favoured - but which would get the go-ahead?

In Brady's public house opinion was divided on the best location. One voice prevailed.

"Whichever way the cards fall it'll do damn all good to you or me. If it's Carlow there's enough men in Carlow to fill the jobs. The same thing in Athy. Either way they're not going to come out here lookin' for men to draw wages."

"They might. There's talk of near on a thousand men bein' wanted in the Winter season, when the crop is drawin' in. There's not that many out of work between the two places."

"There must be damn near enough", a cynic commented.

"No, I'm tellin' you, there's jobs to be had all right."

"They'll probably put it elsewhere at that rate."

*   *   *

In both Athy and Carlow delegations were being organised to lobby for the industry. Farmers were being cajoled into promising a percentage of their acreage to the new crop. Only if the factory management could be sure of local beet growing would they consider siting the factory on the Barrow. And they weren't content with vague promises, they wanted written guarantees of acreage. This would be a major industry. It must succeed.

*   *   *

For Martha Nolan and Thomas Flaherty, the Principals of the girls' and boys' school the Summer brought holidays and a break from the round of teaching. For their charges the long, hot, dry days meant ample time for work on the land and play in the evenings. The village children played in the stream at Carlow Gate or went swimming in the Lerr. Cycling out through the countryside they passed fields of rapidly ripening barley and oats. Week after week stretched hot and dry. In the cracked mud on the edges of the Mill Pond the yellow flags bloomed and withered. The roadside ditches were full of dogroses and poppies. Meadows teemed with oxeye daisies, buttercups and red clover. On the banks of the Lerr and the Griese poachers kept a weather eye open for the Civic Guards. Alder, Beech and Horse Chestnuts were in full leaf along the riverside. Meadows which had flooded in the winter were now drying rapidly - leaving isolated areas of Marsh Marigold - and their rich grasses hid hundreds of snipe. Children picked bunches of Cuckoo flower in fields that had been hidden for most of the winter months. Courting couples cycled to Mullaghcreelan, crossing the brow of the hill, and disappeared into the rich Bluebell carpeted woodland away from the roadway. Elsewhere ditches exploded with Cowparsley, Lesser Celandine, Lesser Periwinkle. It was a Summer to savour.

*   *   *

There were problems too. In several places around the parish, pumps had run dry and people had to travel for miles for fresh water. Every morning Dan MacEvoy inspected the pump on the square, checking the flow of water.

"There's more water wasted testing that pump than'd wash the town", someone quipped.

For Willie Murphy the Summer brought a rest from one of his jobs - School Attendance Officer. But his second source of employment went on. As Relieving Officer for the area he was responsible for looking after the registering and paying of the unemployed. Seasonal work had provided jobs for many men and a few women but the numbers unemployed kept rising.

Kildare County Council had debated the problem at several of the monthly meetings and all kinds of schemes had been proposed but none had brought down the numbers in the dole queues. For Willie Murphy the job went on, week in, week out. There were new faces. Young boys who had left school, worked for a few weeks in temporary jobs on farms, in shops before finding themselves without employment.

"Maybe this new beet factory will ease things", he said.

"Maybe", Mary Hutton said. They were leaning on the wall between their gardens.

"You can never count on these things 'till you see them. It wouldn't be the first time we were told one thing and got another."

Her sister Ann came and joined them.

"Isn't that a glorious evening."

"Grand. With the help of God it'll see us through to the Fraughan fair. Wouldn't it be grand."

"It would."

*   *   *

The "pattern" at Fraughan Hill was held on the second Sunday in July, the twelfth. It was the first pattern there in forty years and its coming had been looked forward to but its popularity had been underestimated. From mid morning on the Sunday cars and bicycles passed through Castledermot as people travelled out to Ballinacarrig, eager to restore the pattern to its former glory. By that afternoon over 2,000 had made their way to the site on Corballis Hill. A committee of younger villagers and parishioners had organised the revival, encouraged and helped by Pat Hennessy and Denis Hayden who remembered the patterns of the previous century.

Denis Hayden opened the Fraughan pattern and welcomed the crowds. He gave a recitation - "Let each man learn to know himself." The Corballis Troupe gave an exhibition of the four hand reel and were followed by Mr. Fitzpatrick of Ballon who also exhibited his skills in dancing. A woman had travelled from Dublin to dance an exhibition hornpipe and an uileann piper had come from Longford to play. The Finlan sisters, from Corballis, sang an Irish duet. A novelty laughing competition was won jointly by Messrs. Doyle of Knocknacree and Galbally of Jerusalem. Mary Cummins of Corballis won the hornpipe competition; the pole and pillow fight was won by Pat Doyle of Belan and the Castledermot Troupe entertained with an Irish chorus. Peter Lacy of Tullow won the sack race and songs were sung by Pat Hennessy, Michael Galbally and Denis Hayden.

As the evening wore on and the two bands who had played through the day prepared to leave it seemed the music would have to end but just in time the Rathvilly Pipe Band arrived and the music and song continued.

Dozens of hawkers sold fruit, sweets and lemonade. A tea tent provided tea, sandwiches and scones - the tent was loaned by Hayden's of Naas. As the evening drew to a close the draw for raffle prizes took place. Ticket 441 was first from the drum, held by Christine Brennan of Baltinglass. Pat

Sommers of Corballis took third prize.

*   *   *

"Wait'll you hear this. Listen to this", the man at Doyle's Bridge folded his copy of the Nationalist to more easily read the article. The men on the wall settled themselves.

"As the day drew to a close one could not but be thankful to God for having lived to see the revival of one of Ireland's ancient pasttimes. Everything that took place on Fraughan Hill was calculated to appeal to the higher aspirations of the soul. One felt that he was living in the higher atmosphere where the air was purer. This was the purer morning air that was to bring Ireland's inevitable day. At Fraughan Hill there was no discordant note; here you were away from the noise and bustle and remorse that so often accompany other gatherings. Here you had no disorder or turmoil, which is the outcome of the excessive use of intoxicating drink. Here the voice of avarice was silent."

The man's audience waited, insuring he had finished.

"By the hokey. Whoever wrote that now wasn't behind you coming home, you and that young one. I seen youse headin' up the Cuckoo steps."

A young man blushed.

"I'd say you were appealing to the higher aspirations of her soul."

"Shut up", another man said urgently. "Here's the Parish Priest."

*   *   *

On the Wednesday and Thursday following the Fraughan festival several people travelled from Castledermot to play in the Carlow open tennis tournament. It cost them 3/6d to enter each event - men's and women's doubles and mixed doubles. For the supporters who travelled with them the admission was 1/-d each or 2/6d per car load. In the grounds of the mental hospital, beside the tennis courts, there were all kinds of stalls - country produce, a treasure hunt, hoop-la and fortune telling. None of the Castledermot players won their way to the finals.

*   *   *

Willie Murphy read with interest the findings of the Department of Education on schools and school attendance in 1923 - the results of which had just been published. The number of pupils had gone up but so too had the average daily attendance of children, from 71.8 to 74.3. This was due. in the main, the report claimed to the appointment of attendance officers. He nodded in agreement as he read the report.

*   *   *

As July wore on two gangs of road men were at work outside Castledermot, tarring the Dublin Road into Castledermot just above the Turnpike and the road to Carlow, beyond Barnhill. The roads were in need of tarring after the heavy Winter and the increased motor traffic. The men worked methodically in the boiling sun, their horse drawn cart moving ahead of them.

*   *   *

The farmers were intensifying their campaign to get the beet factory for the area. In advertisements and posters they urged:

ALL FARMERS ARE EXHORTED TO GROW BEET

They argued that by not securing the beet factory for the Barrow Valley they would lose: £200,000 erection cost for the building itself; work for four hundred to six hundred men every winter; £1,000 a week in wages to factory employees. They argued that getting the factory for the area would give farmers a new cash crop; provide better barley from land which had yielded beet; guarantee a price for the beet crop and provide better prices for butter, poultry and so on. The important point was that 3,000 Irish acres of beet were needed under guarantee. J.J. Bergin, the farmer's organiser in Athy, was busy getting undertakings from land owners in the area. In Castledermot the attitude was more cynical.

"What'd I tell you. There's no question of a thousand jobs. The whole bleddy things is for the benefit of the farmers. Damn all we'll see of it. Look at the facts."

*   *   *

The Irish Independent, in an article in the first week of July, reported that Athy was the favoured site for the new beet factory. Public meetings were held in both Carlow and Athy to lobby for support. The trades union members in both towns were anxious to support the farmers and business people in fighting for their particular area but both towns were united in wanting the factory in the Barrow Valley. In Castledermot the enthusiasm was muted. There might be jobs if the industry got underway, whether it was in Athy or Carlow didn't really matter.

*   *   *

Two recent cases in the local newspaper were causing arguments in the local public houses. In Laois a wealthy woman had drowned in the canal, while in Carlow a man had been charged with attempted suicide.

"It's always the same", one man shouted angrily in Aylmer's. "One law for the rich and another for the poor. If you or me threw ourselves in the river it'd be suicide but if some other people do it it's accidental. Either put the whole lot down for what it is or leave poor simple fellows like your man alone."

"But sure there's no proof that woman did herself in."

"And there's not likely to be. That's the very thing I'm sayin'. It's always hushed up."

*   *   *

Agriculture was the centre of attention all through the fourth week in July. On the 23rd local people flocked to Athy agricultural show. Most of the talk centred on rumours about the imminent announcement of Athy as the site for the sugar factory. On the following day, the 24th, a huge public meeting was held in the Square in Athy. It was announced that 8,000 acres of beet had been guaranteed locally. Meetings and canvasses were held outside all the churches of South Kildare that Sunday morning.

Not only would there be local work on the building and manning of the factory but other jobs were promised too. The Griese was about to be drained. Dozens of men in the Castledermot, Kilkea and Levitstown area would be employed. Those who had been considering emigration thought again. Things seemed to be looking up. And Crookstown Bazaar was coming up, five days of all kinds of events and entertainment from August fifteenth. The month ahead looked good. Perhaps this was not the time to go.

*   *   *

Dozens of local people left Castledermot after early Mass on the 2nd of August, heading for the Leinster senior football semi final between Kildare and Louth: It wasn't a great game but they returned satisfied having seen the home team win by five points. They would meet Wexford or Dublin in the final.

*   *   *

On the following Tuesday John Dunne was among the Labour members at a meeting in Athy to consider the beet factory. The gathering was addressed by a local employer, Mr. Minch. For once, he said, there was common cause between labourer and farmer - employment, an industry for the town. They must work together to make sure it came.

*   *   *

The next day, the first Wednesday in August, was a fair day in Castledermot. Those waking early were surprised by the quietness in the streets. By dawn the village was normally noisy and crowded. This morning there was little stirring. Guard Cosgrave was on early duty. He stood on the Square and chatted with the half dozen horse dealers who had arrived.

"No rush this mornin' hah?"

"No, it's very quiet", the guard said.

"Begod an' if they're not here by now they won't be here at all."

The man was right. There was a very small crowd at the fair. Dublin Horse Show was on and those interested in buying and selling quality horses were there. Only those with agricultural horses had turned up for Castledermot sale and even then prices were low with horses going for between twenty and thirty pounds. Guard MacNamara leaned against the wall at Cope's and smiled, reading the sign painted on MacEvoy's wall: "Teas, Dinners - also monumental works". This was an easier duty than he had expected.

The publicans and caterers, however, were less happy. They had rarely seen such a badly attended fair.

"It should've been changed. What was the sense in havin' it clashin' with the Dublin Show."

"And Athy has a fair day today too."

"We're always the ones as gets left out."

"Ah, well, there'll be a crowd in next Wednesday, for the court. You can sell your pigs and cabbage then!"

*   *   *

The second Sunday in August saw the 108 mile trial organised by Athy Cycle and Car Club. Castledermot was the first checkpoint on the route. The local people took advantage of the fine day to sit out and watch the cars going by. There were Ford and Morris cars and an array of motor cycles and sidecars. Among the cars was the grey and green Morris Cowley. Its driver waved to the people in Castledermot. The young woman he had met from the Dublin train in Maganey sat beside him. They drove out of the village between fields where the reaping was about to begin and other fields where whole crops of turnips had withered in the burning heat of the previous weeks.

At Moone and Timolin and Ballitore there were crowds of people. They sped on along the roads that were sometimes bumpy, sometimes smooth. Here and there cars had been pulled into the ditches, their radiators steaming.

"The advantage of a reliable car", the young driver said.

His passenger smiled.

They passed a motorcyclist, his heavy helmet and goggles glinting in the raw afternoon sun. They enjoyed the shade of trees leaning over the road as they turned in an arc back towards Athy and the end of the run.

*   *   *

As predicted Castledermot was crowded on Wednesday morning for the District Court sitting. And, again, agriculture was in the news. A Tullow farmer who had done threshing work the previous Autumn for a Castledermot farmer was suing for 30/-d which he claimed was owed to him. The local farmer claimed that the Tullow man's thresher was faulty and his workmen were left standing about for hours while the Tullow man attempted to mend a belt on the threshing machine. The Tullow man blamed the quality of hay for the problems with his machine. The Justice, Liam Price, accepted the local man's story but made an award of 10/-d for the work that had been done.

Guard MacNamara, a member of the force in Athy and Inspector of Food and Drink under the Food and Drugs Act was next into the box, prosecuting a Castledermot publican for selling whiskey which was under proof. Kildare County Council, who brought the prosecution, were represented by Mr. Osborne and the defendant by Mr. Law. In evidence the Guard outlined how he had visited the defendant's premises on May 25th and taken samples of whiskey from a cask. The analyst's report was produced. It showed a presence of 3.99% water in the whiskey.

"What did you pay for the whiskey?" Mr. Law asked the Guard.

"I'm not really sure now."

The defendant was called to the stand.

"I had the whiskey in a china jar", he explained. "It wasn't airtight. I remember Guard MacNamara emptying the jar to make up the full sample. I didn't interfere with the whiskey. The fact that the air got at it is the only way I can explain it being under proof. I never touched it."

"Has there ever been any complaint against this publican?", Mr. Law asked the Guard.

"No."

"He's a most respectable trader in the town?"

"Yes, he is."

"The defendant has borne an exceptionally good character, your Honour. I don't think anyone believes he adulterated this whiskey. Rather, it was the effect of the air getting into the container that had the effect.

Mr. Osborne interjected.

"No one says he interfered with the whiskey but we do produce the analyst's report and that shows the drink to be below proof."

Justice Price cut in to end the argument.

"I had a similar case to this one when sitting in Baltinglass. I'll make the same judgement. I'm fining the defendant ten shillings with twenty shillings costs. Next case."

The next case was brought by a man from the Dublin Road who was prosecuting his neighbour for abusive language. The woman had called him a cut throat, he alleged. The defendant agreed that she would not interfere with the man in future and the case was dismissed.

Three men were fined two shillings each for riding bicycles without lights. Another woman was fined two shillings for allowing her cow to wander on the public road and, in the final case of the evening, a local man was fined ten shillings for being drunk and disorderly.

*   *   *

Most evenings of the following week Castledermot was virtually deserted. Those who were on holiday took the bus which left from Hennessy's after lunch. For 1/6d return they could travel to Crookstown Bazaar. In the evening those who had been working cycled out to enjoy the fun.

On Saturday, August 15th, the bazaar was opened by the Parish Priest of Crookstown, Monsignor Wall. This was followed by sports and a clay pigeon shoot and clock golf competition. At half past five a Castledermot team stepped into the boxing enclosure to take part in the tug-o-war competition. They lost the first two pulls of three and retired to watch from the sideline. Some of them stayed on for the ceili which ran until one on Sunday morning.

On the Sunday there were two football matches and a gymnastic display to open the afternoon with the finals of the tug-o-war and another ceili to finish the evening.

On Monday, Moore's betting shop closed in Castledermot and moved, lock, stock and barrel, to Crookstown for the afternoon of horse and pony races. As the racing ended most people headed for the boxing arena where a series of fights was held. Dancing that night was to the Army Number 2 Band.

On Tuesday afternoon there was a motor cycle gymkhana, the final of the clay pigeon shoot was held and a huge crowd gathered at five o'clock for a game of donkey polo. At seven o'clock there was a grand concert and display in the hall, presented by the Association of St. Nicholas. At nine o'clock "Lord Edward's Own Band" took the stage and the dancing began. It went on until five o'clock on Wednesday morning. As with the other dances people had travelled by bus from Athy, Castledermot, the Curragh, Carlow, Naas and Newbridge. A special bus had run each day from O'Connell Bridge in Dublin, bringing dancers and holiday makers to enjoy the festivities.

For many, travelling on the bus from Castledermot, the new burning topic of conversation was photography. Several people in the village had bought cameras and were comparing notes. Most had taken their cameras with them to the bazaar, searching for a good photograph.

"Well, photographs or no photographs", one farm worker said, travelling home at half past five on the Wednesday morning, "it's back to work now. The harvest'll be starting tomorrow. We can forget about dancing and photographs for the next couple of weeks."

"You never know", his friend said. "This time next year we might all have cushy jobs in the beet factory in Athy."

"Is it given to Athy?"

"No, but it will be. They're announcing it next week. It said Athy was getting it in the paper."

"I don't know. I think I'd rather be out in the fresh air than stuck in some factory. I think I'll stay where I am."

*   *   *

With the weather still up the threshing machines were trundling along the roadways earlier each morning, moving from field to field and farm to farm. School children on the last day of their holiday, were busy side by side with their mothers and fathers, in the fields. Work began at dawn and went on until dusk and after it.

"We'll get this one finished", farmers shouted. "We might as well get it done."

In farmhouses huge pots of potatoes and cabbage and bacon were boiled and presented to the crowds of hungry reapers. At mid morning and mid afternoon men took short breaks to drink cold tea or buttermilk. All the time the engines thundered on the threshing machines. Children who had no work to do sat on the ditches and watched the rabbits and rats race from the fields as the reaping progressed.

At Cope's mill the men were working overtime. Trailer loads of barley were drawn up in both directions from the gates. The wheel turned regularly as the sacks were piled in all corners. The tractor and lorry drivers smoked and laughed as they waited in line.

"What about Kildare on Sunday?"

"They'll get there all right."

"Wexford are no push over."

"I'd say they won't be that good."

"Are you going?"

"It all depends on the way the harvesting goes. If we get it all in by Saturday I will. If not we'll be working on Sunday too. You can't take a risk with the weather."

In other fields on other farms the harvesting was being done by horse drawn harvesters. The horses worked slowly, cutting swathes up and down the fields, starting before the sun came up and making their way home after darkness had fallen. All over the parish men were leaving their homes before light and only getting home long after night had fallen.

*   *   *

Despite the work and the fine weather there were dozens of people in Maganey on the Sunday morning for the train to Dublin to see Kildare and Wexford play in the Leinster senior football final. The train was overcrowded. People who had paid full fair had to stand, crushed, in the guard's van.

"This happens every bleddy year. They know there's going to be a crowd but they won't put on extra carriages."

In Athy things got worse with dozens more pushing their way on board. But, overall, the mood was good. This could be the year for the Lily Whites. They had a good team, they could go all the way and win the All Ireland Final. Wexford would be a good test but no more than that.

For those coming back into Castledermot that night, in cars or cycling from Maganey station, the mood was subdued. Kildare had failed to spark. Wexford had never really been in trouble and had won quite easily, 2-7 to 0-5.

"They're not worth a bleddy curse. They wouldn't kick butter."

*   *   *

For the young boy who had applied, unsuccessfully, for the job as shepherd at Cope's of Knocknagee life as a worker with horses was becoming more acceptable. True, he was very busy with the harvesting but he was beginning to develop a liking for the horses and an ability to know when to do what. He was responsible, now, for seeing that all the horses working through the harvest were fit and well. There was no time for them to graze, they were in harness most of the time. And they needed more nourishment with the heavy work that had to be done. The boy had a rota of feeding to get through each day. The cart horses were looked after while standing at the stack. Forksfull of green, second-cut, clover were brought down to them. A few handsfull of corn were thrown in to keep them going.

Three times a day he brought corn to the horses in the binder and, occasionally, a feed of maize and cracked peas. With the continuing hot weather the boy also carted buckets of water with one or two hands of oatmeal stirred in to slake the horses' thirst.

Watching the tractors and machinery on some of the farms as he cycled home he wondered if he'd ever get to drive them.

*   *   *

A new assistant for Cope's hardware had arrived in Castledermot on the last Saturday of the month. He had come on the train to Maganey and cycled in, his suitcase strapped to the back of his bicycle. Stopping at the houses in Woodlands he had enquired about lodgings. A woman directed him to Willie Byrne, the saddler's, in Main Street.

*   *   *

With the Winter approaching and the new school year beginning Willie Murphy, the Relieving and School Attendance Officer, walked down to Billy Hoey's to be measured for a pair of shoes.

"We won't feel the Winter in now", Billy said. "Once the fine weather goes that'll be the end of the Summer."

"We can't complain all the same. It was a good Summer."

"It was but I hope we don't have a Winter like the last one."

"Ah, sure you never know what's ahead", Willie Murphy said.

*   *   *

At a meeting of the I.T.& G.W.U. in Athy on the last Friday night of the August of 1925 a delegation was appointed to meet the Belgian, Mr. Lippens, who would finally decide on the location of the new beet factory. They wanted nothing left to chance. As they were meeting word came through that the announcement had been made. The new sugar beet factory would be sited in the Barrow Valley - in Carlow.

*   *   *

With the disappointment of the Leinster football final beginning to fade local enthusiasts were now looking forward to the first Sunday in September when Kildare would meet Kerry in a challenge match in Athy. In the week before the game it was postponed indefinitely.

*   *   *

On that Sunday morning the Parish Priest in Castledermot, like many Parish Priests in the area, spoke on the subject of children returning to school. He addressed himself particularly to the subject of modesty and urged parents of girls returning to school to ensure their children's dresses were not too short. Many girls, he said, were wearing dresses immodestly short. He hoped he would not have to deal with this problem again.

*   *   *

It was noticeable that several faces were missing from the church that Sunday morning. The harvest was drawing to a close. Carlow would employ Carlow people, it wasn't just a different town, it was a different county. There'd be little or no work for Castledermot men there. The boat to England was the answer. Several young men had left in the last few weeks, heading mainly for Birmingham. They promised they'd be home for Christmas.

"Now where did we hear that one before?" Tommy Dwyer remarked sarcastically.

* * *

On Monday morning Martha Nolan made her way from her house on Main Street to the rat infested girls' school on the corner of Church Lane. Tomas Flaherty was, at the same time, opening the boys' school at the other end of the School Lane. The Summer was surely over now, Martha Nolan thought. Once school opened that was it.

* * *

Out on Greene's farm two of the workmen were drawing barley.

"I see Grangecon bet yis", one of them laughed. "What was it? Forty three runs?"

"We were short two good men."

"Kilkea are always short something."

"We'll see how youse do next week."

"I'll tell you now", the first man said. "Levitstown will bury them. Wait'll you see."

"Tell me that next Monday morning", the Kilkea man said.

"I will", the other man said. He played for Levitstown cricket club.

* * *

A special practice match for the local football team had been advertised for the Fair Green. 'An important meeting will follow', the notice read. Mrs. Abbot watched the men and boys from her house overlooking the Green. She was glad to see them back playing there. It was company to see them all gathered, kicking up between the two sets of coats that formed the goalposts.

"If they won't come up to Barnhill we'll have to bleddy bring the practice down here", one of the older men watching the game muttered. "It wouldn't have happened an' I playin'."

* * *

Children who had seen posters for Barry's circus in Athy that first week in September waited each morning for the tent to appear in Gannon's field but it didn't stop in Castledermot.

*   *   *

The Seanad elections came on September 17th. There was little canvassing and less interest in Castledermot. Thirty five per cent of the people turned out to vote on the day. The figure was slightly higher in Athy but not much.

*   *   *

The price of barley was down to twenty to twenty five shillings a barrel. No price had been set at the start of the season and now the farmers were complaining about the prices being paid. Their wrath was directed not at the companies paying them but at the government.

*   *   *

"I suppose electricity is the next thing we'll see in the church?", Dr. Brannon asked leaning out of his car as the Parish Priest passed.

"Why do you say that?"

"Well they have it in the church in Athy now. Can Castledermot be far behind?"

"We'll see. We'll see."

*   *   *

"What did I tell you?", the Levitstown man shouted cycling through the rain into Greene's farmyard.

"What?"

"Didn't I tell you we'd beat Grangecon."

"What did yis win by?"

"Fifty six runs to thirty seven. Now where's all the talk about Kilkea?"

The rain was back and it continued to rain heavily through the last week in September.

IV

Autumn / Winter

John MacKenna

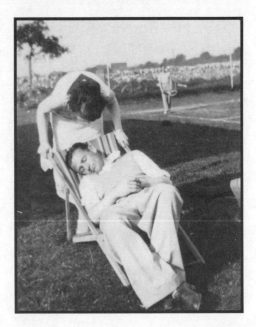

As Autumn came so did a change in the weather. The fine days and warm nights were gone. It seemed the Winter of 1925 would be like that of 1924 - cold and wet.

The October fair in the village saw a large turnout of horses with the big dealers back in attendance. Good blood stock was fetching reasonable prices but agricultural horses remained low. Three year old draught horses were selling from £14 to £16 and four year olds from £17 to £22. With the hunting season opening there was a large supply of good hunters and demand was high, pushing the prices up. A handful of really good quality hunters changed hands for £150 each.

The Square and the Main Street were crowded with horses. Down towards Keenan's Lane there were pens of cattle and sheep. Business was slow enough with these. Prices were steady and unlikely to go up or down too much.

The upcoming all night carnival dance at the new hall on October 21st was the social occasion most people were looking forward to. Every Sunday night there were practice dances with the Castledermot Dance Band playing. They were always well attended.

*   *   *

On the second Tuesday in October there was a flurry of excitement as a convoy of Civic Guards was seen taking two men - one from Belan and one from Killelan - to Liam Dalton's house. Dalton was a Peace Commissioner. The two men had climbed over the back wall of the Leinster Arms Hotel in the Square on the previous Sunday night and taken a motor pump, a tyre and other bits and pieces for a car from the yard of the building. The men were arrested on Tuesday and taken to Dalton's where a special court was held. Both men were released on bail to be brought before the District court on the following Wednesday week.

*   *   *

Out on the Griese work had been underway for several weeks on drainage and clearing. Almost a hundred men from Castledermot, Moone, Kilkea and Levitstown were working on the project, widening and deepening the channel and clearing away the overgrowth on the banks. There was talk of work beginning, at last, on the Barrow drainage once the Griese was clear.

"A lot of youse can expect work on that", the foreman told them. "Once youse have the knack from working here the jobs'll be there on the Barrow."

*   *   *

The young man in the Morris Cowley stopped on the bridge at Kilkea to admire the work the men were doing. The river swept wide and clean into the trees that hid Kilkea Castle from the roadway. He was on his way to Athy to collect his dress suit for the Motor Club dance on October 23rd.

*   *   *

The third Wednesday in October saw the usual collection of uneasy, baffled and wary faces outside the courthouse. Justice Price parked his car in the yard of the Leinster Arms and the Sergeant accompanied him into the courthouse. Twenty minutes later the first case was being heard.

George Jackson, the owner of a garage in Carlow, was being summoned by Guard Halloran in a technical case. Jackson had allowed a load of Mex petrol to be delivered in one of his lorries to Cope's without the lorry being licenced under the Trade Act to carry such a consignment.

"Jasus, they've little to be doin' with their time". a man at the back of the court whispered to the woman beside him. She nodded.

Guard Halloran took the stand and explained how he'd found Jackson's lorry being driven from Carlow to Castledermot with a quantity of petrol. Jackson could only produce a limited trade licence and this didn't allow him to carry petrol. Jackson was called and told the Justice his company was building a new body for the lorry and he had allowed his mechanic to drive the lorry to Castledermot to oblige Shell Mex who wanted the petrol brought to Cope's pump.

"The regulations in England allow a garage man to do that," Jackson said.

"The regulations you're referring to do not apply in this country", Justice Price snapped.

"He put his foot in it there", the man at the back whispered.

"I didn't get paid for this", Jackson went on. "I didn't know I was breaking the regulations."

The Justice considered the charge.

"I could make an order", he said. "I'm satisfied this whole thing was a misunderstanding. I could make an order for you to appeal."

Jackson looked unhappy.

"Will you give me an undertaking not to let this happen again?" the Justice asked.

Jackson agreed that he would.

"Very well. I'll mark the case as a caution to you."

Guard Halloran was involved in the following case as well.. He had summoned Michael Ryan, a veterinary surgeon from Abbeyleix, for driving a Ford car at Castledermot while the licence was out of date.

Ryan was in court and was called to the stand.

"I fractured my arm a while back", he explained. The Justice seemed unimpressed.

"I had to go to Dublin for treatment. The car was left lying up and the licence went out of date. When I got home I got an urgent call out to Castledermot and I took out the car. I got a licence two days after the guard stopped me. I hadn't the slightest intention of evading the regulations."

The Justice informed him that the maximum penalty he could impose was a fine of three times the annual licence duty.

"That's £18", he said. "So I am entitled to fine you £54."

Ryan blanched.

"However, I will mitigate that to a fine of £1."

The next case concerned a local man who owed £12.10s. to a local shopkeeper. When the case was called the man did not appear. The Justice made an order against the man for £12.10s. plus 9/10d interest.

"The next case is a long one, your honour. It concerns a serious assault," Guard Halloran told the Justice.

"Very well, we'll take it after lunch."

*　　　*　　　*

Out in the streets business was going on as usual. In the new hall local women were putting the final touches to the decorations for that night's all night dance. Boxes of sandwiches were being brought into the supper room. A girl was sprinkling glitter on the dance floor.

*　　　*　　　*

After lunch two brothers from Corballis were in the dock, charged with seriously assaulting a man from Ballyhackett on August 15th.

In reply to Superintendent Kelly, the man who had been assaulted said that on the fifteenth of August he had been driving with the defendants and three other men in a car they had hired from Mr. Hennessy. Mr. Hennessy was driving and was accompanied by his son, a young boy. They drove to the home of the defendants in Corballis and while they were waiting outside in the car a row started in the house. One of the defendants came out of the house and ordered the boy from the car. The witness tried to stop him and a tussle began. The witness was thrown to the ground. While he was on the ground the defendant kicked him in the face, resulting in a deep cut under his left eye. The guards arrived and took him to the doctor in Castledermot. As far as he was concerned only one of the brothers was involved, the man who had kicked him. The second brother had nothing to do with the assault. A second witness was called. He had been in the car with the last witness and the defendants.

"I went up the town that day", he told the Justice. "Unfortunately, I had a few pints. I went for the drive when Mr. Hennessy was leaving the brothers to Corballis. When we got there Mr. Hennessy was paid and then one of the brothers asked to be driven to Baltinglass. I didn't go near the shambles at all. I saw several people pushing one another. I saw the last witness striking the defendant."

Edward Hennessy, the car driver, was then called. He told how he had been hired to drive the brothers to Corballis.

"When we got there one of them asked me to drive him to Baltinglass. I said I wanted to get home because I had a child with me. The second brother didn't want to go to Baltinglass at all. I told the fellow who did to leave the child in the car and be ready to start. He then caught me by the coat but I didn't see him hitting the first witness."

"Had he much drink taken?" the Justice asked.

"He had enough. They were all fairly merry."

Guard Halloran gave evidence of arriving at the scene and finding one of the brothers, the one alleged to have done the kicking, lying at his gateway, under the influence of drink. He went over to Mr. Hennessy's car and found three men in it. The first witness had a dangerous cut under his left eye. He asked who had inflicted the wound but the witness would not tell him then. He brought the first witness and the defendant to Castledermot. The doctor dressed the man's wound and Guard Halloran then arrested the defendant.

The defendant interrupted from the dock.

"I was in the war and when I get a few drinks I lose my head."

Superintendent Kelly asked the Justice to take a very serious view of the case.

"The conduct of these men on a church holy day was scandalous", the Justice remarked. "There is no evidence against the first of the brothers and I will let him off. But I am sentencing the second brother to one month's imprisonment, with hard labour, for common assault."

The brothers parted without any acknowledgement, one being led away, the other returning to the body of the court.

"I wonder did he bring a change of clothes itself", the man at the back of the court whispered.

The cases that followed were an anticlimax.

Four farmers from Davidstown, Woodlands, Prumplestown and Belan were summoned for failing to have noxious weeds on their lands cut.

The Inspector for the Minister for Lands told how he had visited the farm at Davidstown and found most of the 600 acres in a bad state with thistles. He served the owner with a notice to have them cut. Returning the following month he found only 25 acres had been cut. The result was that the adjoining lands would be infested with thistles at seeding time.

The steward on the farm told the Justice it had cost £40 to have the weeds cut. The Inspector claimed the weeds could be cut in three weeks.

"There's no labour to be got", the steward said.

"There are a lot of people unemployed in this area", the Inspector said.

The farmer was fined £5.

The farmer from Woodlands claimed he always cut his lands. The 70 acres involved were not nearly as bad as the Inspector claimed.

He was fined £2 with £1 expenses.

The farmer from Belan claimed the Inspector had not carried out an inspection of his land at all.

"With the fine weather I had no time to cut thistles before the date laid down", he told the Justice. "I was busy getting in the hay crop."

"The lands are in a bad state", the Inspector replied. "It took me three quarters of an hour to walk them."

Again, the Justice fined £2 with £1 expenses.

The Prumplestown owner claimed that the summons served was in the name of his father while he was the owner of the land. His case was dismissed.

A Dunlavin man was charged with failing to halt when called on by a Guard in Castledermot. He was further charged with having no light on his car and with having no driving licence.

He explained that he hadn't heard the Guard call on him to halt. The charge was dismissed but he was fined £1 on the other two charges.

Two minor cases followed, one for cycling with no light and the second for allowing a cow to wander on the public road. In each case the fine was two shillings.

Another serious case brought the days sitting to a close.

Percy Whitmore told of being assaulted on 21st September by a man with firearms. He was threatened by the armed man and given seven days to leave the district. He reported the matter to the Guards at Castledermot.

Sergeant Scott took up the story. He told of being given a description of the man with the gun. In the description it was said that the man involved had had candle grease on his clothes. The Sergeant had suspected a man from Hughestown. He arrested the man and, on searching his house, found clothes with candle grease. At an identification parade at Castledermot station on September 22nd Percy Whitmore had identified the accused.

The Justice sentenced the Hughestown man to a calendar month in jail, with hard labour. He was also ordered to enter into a bond of good behaviour for twelve months with a surety of £20 from himself and an independent surety of £20.

*   *   *

Out in the streets it was dark and people were hurrying home from work. The police van pulled away from the courthouse on its way to Mountjoy. The Justice drove his car out of the Leinster Arms yard.

Among the three hundred people at the all night dance there was much talk of the heavy sentences handed out to the two men who had gone to jail.

*   *   *

The man in the Morris Cowley was among the huge crowd at the Motor Club dance in the Legion Hall in Athy the following Friday night. Many people were in fancy dress. An all night buffet was running in the supper room. The Selma Follies Band from Dublin were playing on the bandstand. At half past eleven the fancy dress parade was held. The results would be announced and the prizes presented at two o'clock. Two Guards who had looked in on the dance decided not to wait. They left the hall and were on their way back to the barracks when they noticed a gate in St. John's Lane open. They went through the gate, onto waste ground. Guard MacNamara shone his torch along a wall and was confronted by three men hiding in a corner. He called on them to halt as they began to run away and one of them turned and fired three shots from a revolver. The two guards chased the men but they escaped into a quarry. The Guards returned to the hall and warned the men on the door. A search of local houses was begun and three masks were found near the wall. The men were not caught.

The man in the Morris Cowley decided to leave. His girlfriend and he returned to the car and drove down Duke Street and Leinster Street and onto the Castledermot Road. The girl was very nervous.

"These things happen", the man said. "But it's better to get away from it."

*　　*　　*

Castledermot was full of talk about the shooting next day.

"There's a few guns around still", Joe Kinsella said, leaning against his door. "And there's a fair few boys know how to use them."

The two men on the path outside nodded.

"They were lucky not to get shot."

"There's no sense in unarmed men takin' on fellows with guns", one of the men said.

The Parish Priest passed and the men raised their caps. They waited until he was out of earshot and resumed their conversation.

*　　*　　*

The fine weather and the early harvest meant that the tilling of the land was well underway. Dozens of pairs of plough horses were on the roads and in the fields. Here and there tractors roared around corners or thudded through the freshly turned soil. In Stanley's and Wall and Butler's forges the bright fires dazzled the passing children in the dank, twilit evenings. Some of them, passing on their way for milk or messages, stood tentatively in the doorways, watching the blaze and listening to the men chatting as they waited for shoeing or plough repairs to be finished.

In the dimly lit Cope and Torry shop women bought wool and needles for the dark evenings of knitting. Jimmy Loughlin was busy delivering loads of turf, heeling up his cart in backyards. In Hoey's and Lawlor's the sound of nails being tapped into leather continued late into the night. Only those with warm coats gathered at the bridge in the evening. Card schools were starting again in houses throughout the parish. Winter was setting in.

*   *   *

On the afternoon of the last Thursday in October Willie Murphy completed his business, collected his bicycle from the courthouse and cycled slowly out of Athy. It was a cold, clear afternoon and he was looking forward to a leisurely journey home, in particular the walk up Mullaghcreelan where the trees would be laden with crab apples. Going out through Ardreigh Murphy saw a movement in a clump of bushes and seconds later he was fired on. The shots missed him and he cycled as fast as he could, waiting for further shots or a call to halt, but neither came. He considered going back into Athy to report the matter but thought it safer to continue. Getting to Castledermot he contacted Sergeant Scott who notified the Guards in Athy. Several houses in the area were searched and on the following Sunday evening an arms dump was found in a hay loft in Fortbarrington. The Guards recovered 20 sticks of gelignite, a .32 revolver and a .303 rifle and a large collection of ammunition.

In Castledermot Willie Murphy was the centre of attention. There were several callers to his house and after Mass on the Sunday he found himself relating the story for the hundredth time to a large crowd outside the church.

On the Monday, when word of the arms find had spread, Tommy Dwyer met Willie Murphy on the Square.

"Isn't it lucky now", Dwyer said. "They used the gun on you and missed. You might not have got off so handy if they brought the gelignite and tossed that after you."

Murphy laughed.

"You're right", he said.

*   *   *

Another special court was held in Castledermot on November 2nd. A Ballyburn man had been found in possession of a wardrobe of clothes which he didn't own. He was refused bail and transferred to Mountjoy to await trial at Tullow court.

The nights were too cold and wet in November for men to gather at Cope's Corner or Doyle's Bridge. Instead they met in public houses or in the billiard hall or at card games in houses. The village had become quiet, like the countryside around it, settling into Winter.

"I'll tell you one thing", Peter Hearns said, lifting his hand of cards. "Rain or no rain and rough road or not there's one bad thing about the doing up of the Carlow Road, the cars coming down Barnhill are flying. And they're flying through the town. There's someone going to be killed yet with the way they're travelling."

Mrs. Giltrap nodded.

"I see Price complaining about that very thing in the paper. He's threatening to push up the fines. There's a run of people being caught for fast driving."

*　　　*　　　*

Some of the men working on the lower reaches of the Griese were called in during the middle week of November and asked to help with a search on the Barrow for a twenty three year old Mountrath man who was missing. They spent a day searching the banks and the river but nothing was found.

The Carrickford Theatre Company took over the new hall for the third week in November and presented Sir Hall Caine's "The Boardsman." The hall was packed to the doors on the opening night and there were good crowds through the rest of the week.

"There's a thing that'll disappear now", Mrs. Thorpe said, leaning on the Post Office counter. "With the new hall open."

"What's that?" Mrs. Cross asked.

"The travelling shows putting up in Gannon's field. There wasn't one this year. They'll all be in the hall now. You'd miss the feeling that used to be in the tents for shows."

*　　　*　　　*

Through the last fortnight in November and the first week of December the village was busy every night with groups and individuals rehearsing for the concert due on the eighth of December. It was to be a most impressive affair and a huge crowd was guaranteed.

In the boys' and girls' schools the choirs were taken each afternoon and put through their paces. The curate, Fr. Tim Condon, spent a great deal of time checking and re-checking that people would take part and would be prepared. He arranged for musicians to travel from Baltinglass and then called on the school teachers to encourage the children's choirs. In houses around the parish individuals were polishing their acts. Dr. Brannon's daughters were preparing a cello and piano duet. Hennessy's was particularly busy as the local dancing troupe rehearsed.

*　　　*　　　*

At the Athy Farmers Union dance their friends congratulated the man with the Morris Cowley and his fiancée on their engagement. They planned to marry in the Spring. At the same dance John Greene was busy talking to local farmers, urging them to commit themselves to a larger acreage of beet for the new factory. Carlow was the site but work would not begin until the farmers had signed agreements for guaranteed acreage and there was a shortfall of several hundred guaranteed acres. He moved around the edges of the dance floor and across the supper room talking to people, impressing on them the importance of completing the growing guarantee in the next few weeks.

*　　　*　　　*

The new hall was thronged for the concert on the eighth of December. As soon as the Parish Priest had taken his seat the evening began. The Diocesan examiner, Fr. Michael Murphy, gave a talk on Lourdes, illustrated by slides. Those at the back of the hall grew restless as the lecture went on and when Fr. Murphy turned to the 1924 pilgrimage there was some tittering and talk from those standing near the door. The Parish Priest looked sternly about, trying to pinpoint the culprits but the lecturer realised that he was in danger of outstaying his welcome and brought his talk to an end.

The concert proper began with Mae Hennessy singing "Ave Maria." The Brannon girls played their duet and were followed by a vocal group from Baltinglass - led by Dr. Schofield. Mary Lawlor of Pill received a great hand when she sang, "Why don't my dreams come true", and was called back for an encore. Mae Hennessy made a second appearance and was followed onstage by the girls' school choir who sang, "Eamon an Cnoic". The boys' choir was conducted by Tomás Flaherty and Mae Hennessy and the Castledermot troupe of dancers brought the night to a rousing conclusion. The Parish Priest thanked everyone present for their support. Some boys standing near the back door shifted uneasily from foot to foot as he stared at them but he said nothing. Doubtless they'd be waylaid in the street during the week.

"Mind you're not shot at going home", one of them called to Willie Murphy as he left the hall.

It was a frosty night and the roads glistened in the lights of bicycle lamps. Sergeant Scott stood in the Square, watching the crowds disperse. He jiggled his feet to keep some life in his freezing toes.

*   *   *

Shops were busy from the 8th onwards, with a brisk Christmas trade It seemed Castledermot would have a bumper month of shopping. On the 16th of December, however, almost a hundred men from the parish, who had been working on the Lerr drainage scheme and drawing 30/-d a week each in wages, were let go. Four thousand pounds had been spent on the scheme and a further £300 remained of the budget. The weather was given as the reason for ending the scheme and there were promises of more work in the Spring of 1926. For the men coming home that evening, however, Spring was a distant prospect. Christmas was a week away. The money they had expected to draw in Christmas week was gone and the early part of the new year would be bleak. There was no work on the land and wasn't likely to be for months.

"They know how to pick their time", one of the workers said, wheeling his bicycle into the village.

"I heard Henry, the Board of Works fellow, saying there'd be more work done in Hughestown in the new year. He said there's talk of an extended grant to finish up the job," his companion sympathised.

"I'll tell my young wans that." the man said. "That'll cheer them up over the Christmas. I'll tell them Santa Claus will be coming at Easter."

*   *   *

In the same week three dozen people turned up at a meeting in the girl's school to hear P.J. Scollan explain the benefits of setting up a branch of the Town Tenants' Association. A branch would help Castledermot, he told his audience, giving the residents a united voice and a means of getting things done. Most people in the room enrolled as members and paid their subscriptions and a meeting was arranged for early in January.

*   *   *

On the afternoon of the school holidays the girls in the national school had a short concert. Two men sat on the wall outside, waiting to collect their daughters, listening to the children singing:

> Oh see the white snowflakes how gently they fall,
> like pretty wee stars they come down,
> not straight like the raindrops but dancing about,
> I see there are some on the ground.

"That's all we need now", one of the men commented to the large group of women nearby.

"God forbid", one of them said.

*　　　*　　　*

There were choir practices every night in the Catholic Church, the Christmas carols were rehearsed under the direction of Tomas Flaherty. In St. James' the choir met to rehearse the music for the Christmas day service. The curate, Fr. Condon, was informed that he would be moving to Clondalkin in the new year. The heavy frost of the previous weeks turned to bitter, endless rain. It was a grey, depressed Christmas. There was the grand Christmas dance to look forward to on December 27th and the new year. There might be more work then.

Two children playing in the Square sang a school song:

> Hi, ho, holly and mistletoe,
> now it's December and Christmas is near,
> soon comes the day we are longing for,
> happiest day in the whole of the year.

Martha Nolan came out of Cope and Torry's, carrying a small parcel. She smiled at the children. There was a crowd in Giltraps. Willie Byrne, Tommy Dwyer and Daisy Dent stood outside MacEvoy's, chatting. Jimmy Loughlin passed in his horse and cart.

"A happy Christmas to yis", he shouted.

"And the same to you."

Catherine Hayden came out of Cope's. She was followed by two children carrying a shopping bag between them.

"Will this rain ever lift?", she commented, passing Mrs. Farrelly outside Thompsons.

It was getting dark. People were making for home. It was Christmas Eve. There was still a lot of work to be done.

V

Epilogue

John MacKenna

The young boy who had hoped to be a shepherd stayed with his horses for another year and then followed his sisters to Birmingham.

The horses themselves became scarce, their huge feathered feet no longer pounded down the overgrown country roads.

The fires went out in the village forges and the music stopped in the new hall, its doors re-opened to house sparkling motor cars at a price that every family could afford.

Sam Browne's congregation dwindled and his sermons grew less frequent.

Billy Hoey left his shoemaking and moved to Dublin where he was killed.

The cricket club at Hallahoise declined, the crease became overgrown and the only movement was the shadows from the evergreens at the end of the field, stirring in the evening breeze.

The young man in the Morris Cowley married his fiancée. In the autumn of 1926 she died in childbirth. Twelve days later her infant son was buried beside her.

Other families came, new shops were opened, public houses changed hands, new schools were built but the community of 1925 became, eventually, part of a lost village, replaced by new people, a new town.